C000205478

T·H·E B·E·S·T O·F
STRAWBERRIES

SELECT
EDITIONS

CLB 4446
Published 1995 by CLB Publishing
Exclusively for Selectabook Ltd, Devizes
© 1995 CLB Publishing, Godalming, Surrey
ISBN 1-85833-327-X

Printed and bound in Italy

CONTENTS

INTRODUCTION

The appearance of the first strawberries is a sure sign that summer has arrived. According to the writings of Ovid, Pliny and Virgil, they were already well known in the Roman world. Much later, it was recorded that Henry VIII of England had paid 10 shillings for a 'pottle' of strawberries. But in spite of their obvious popularity, these fruits must have been rather miserable specimens compared with the cultivated ones we have today. Attempts were made to breed better strains, but the real breakthrough did not come about until the nineteenth century, when two species imported from the New World, *Fragaria chilensis* and *Fragaria virginiana*, met by accident in France. Since then, the strawberry has never looked back.

In addition to the usual garden varieties, there is also the alpine strawberry, a miniature plant that produces fruit throughout the summer. Although it has been cultivated for centuries, it has so far resisted all attempts to make it grow any bigger. Smallest of all are the wild strawberries which grow in grassy woods from the end of June to August, and have the sweetest and most highly flavoured berries of all.

When buying strawberries, look for fresh, clean fruit with bright green hulls and stems. As with other soft fruits, avoid washing if possible. If necessary clean them lightly as follows. Lay the berries in a single layer on a cloth wrung out of cold water, roll the cloth up loosely and shake gently. Any grit or dust is transferred to the damp cloth, leaving the fruit clean. As a last resort, wash strawberries by floating a single layer in a large bowl of cold water. Swish the water gently with your hand, leave it for a minute to allow any grit to sink to the bottom, then quickly transfer the fruit to a colander to drain. Strawberries should always be cleaned or washed before they are hulled.

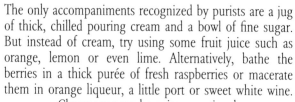

The only accompaniments recognized by purists are a jug of thick, chilled pouring cream and a bowl of fine sugar. But instead of cream, try using some fruit juice such as orange, lemon or even lime. Alternatively, bathe the berries in a thick purée of fresh raspberries or macerate them in orange liqueur, a little port or sweet white wine. Champagne can be quite sensational.

Make the most of strawberries while they last. Apart from jams, which are a great favourite, they do not make particularly good preserves. Unless you like crunching the berries in a semi-frozen state, freezing can be disappointing as the fruit turns flabby and loses its brightness when thawed. To avoid this, use small to medium-sized berries and freeze them in a thick raspberry purée so that the juices which the strawberries release as they thaw automatically blend with the purée. Alternatively, crush the strawberries to a pulp before freezing them, ready to use in other recipes.

A final warning. Strawberries have little natural pectin so more will have to be added in the form of lemon or redcurrant juice, or bottled pectin, if a jam is to set properly. This is especially important if frozen fruit is used. Strawberries are both delicious and good for you. They are particularly high in Vitamin C and folic acid, and also have significant quantities of iron, calcium and phosphorus.

WILD STRAWBERRY SOUP

---

450 grams (1 lb) wild strawberries
About 100-125 grams (4 oz) sugar
2 egg yolks
150 millilitres (¼ pint) thick cream
Lemon juice (optional)
Sugared croûtons or puffed wheat cereal, to garnish

Pick over and rinse strawberries if necessary. Mix them with the sugar and either purée in an electric blender or food processor, or crush to a purée with a fork. Dilute with about 1 litre (1¼–1¾ pints) cold water. Pour into a pan and heat gently, stirring to dissolve any remaining sugar.

Beat egg yolks lightly with cream. Beat in a few tablespoons of the hot, puréed soup. Pour back into pan of soup and stir constantly over low heat until it thickens. Take great care not to let it boil or egg yolks will curdle. Taste soup and add a little more sugar or a squeeze of lemon juice if liked. Soup may be served either hot or cold; if the latter, cool and chill it lightly first. Serve garnished with sugared croûtons or puffed wheat cereal.

Serves 6

HONEYED
STRAWBERRIES

For about 700 grams (1½ lbs) strawberries, which will serve 4–6, prepare the following syrup. In a wide saucepan, dissolve 4 tablespoons runny honey and 2 tablespoons sugar in 150 millilitres (¼ pint) water. (Use mild honey for this. A strong honey would get in the way of the flavour of the strawberries.) Add a strip of lemon peel and simmer for 5 minutes.

Add strawberries to the simmering syrup and cook gently for 5 minutes before switching off the heat. Allow to cool to lukewarm before serving.

SOYER'S STRAWBERRY SALAD

From Alexis Soyer's *Shilling Cookery for the People* (1855).

'A large pottle (basket) of ripe strawberries, picked (i.e. hulled) and put into a basin with two tablespoonfuls of sugar, a pinch of powdered cinnamon, a gill of brandy (or a few tablespoons liqueur, wine or fruit juice); stir gently, and serve.
'Currants and raspberries the same.'

STRAWBERRY AND CURRANT SALAD

From Mrs Bowman's *New Cookery Book* (1867).

'A pretty dessert dish may be made of mixed early fruits, strawberries, white or red currants, gooseberries and cherries, all carefully picked, placed in alternate layers strewed with sugar, and piled up with taste. Either simple cream, or wine or brandy cream, should be poured over the salad.'

STRAWBERRIES IN LIME CREAM SAUCE

450 grams (1 lb) strawberries
4 tablespoons fresh lime juice
About 2 tablespoons sifted icing sugar

Lime cream sauce
3 egg yolks
100–125 grams (4 oz) caster sugar
225 millilitres (8 fl. oz) single cream
Thinly peeled rind of ½ lime
100–125 millilitres (4 fl. oz) double cream

Start by preparing the sauce. In the top of a double saucepan (or a heat-proof bowl that will fit snugly over a pan of simmering water), beat egg yolks and sugar together until fluffy. In a heavy pan, scald single cream with the lime-rind, peeled off with a potato peeler. Off the heat, pour gradually into the egg yolks and sugar, stirring vigorously with a wooden spoon. Fit top of pan or bowl over simmering water and cook, stirring until custard is thick enough to coat back of spoon. Take care not to let it boil, or egg yolks will curdle. Leave until quite cold, stirring occasionally to prevent a skin forming on top.

Finally, remove and discard the strip(s) of lime rind. Shortly before serving, beat double cream until thick and fold in lime custard sauce. Chill lightly.

Clean strawberries on a damp cloth or rinse them briefly if necessary. Hull them and halve or quarter any large ones so that they are all of the same size. In a bowl, toss strawberries gently with lime juice and sifted icing sugar, to taste. Cover bowl and chill lightly until ready to serve.

To serve, turn strawberries over in their juices once more and divide between 4 individual glass serving bowls. Spoon lime cream sauce over each bowl and serve immediately.

Serves 4

SHERRIED STRAWBERRIES

900 grams (2 lbs) fresh, ripe strawberries, cleaned and hulled
175–225 grams (6–8 oz) sugar
Sherry

Put alternate layers of strawberries and sugar in a wide-necked jar, filling the jar right up to the top. Pour in the sherry until the fruit is covered. Do this very slowly so that no air bubbles are formed.

If any bubbles remain trapped in the jar, release them by slipping a flat knife blade down the side of the jar. Be careful, though, not to pierce the fruit while doing so.

Seal tightly and store.

FRAGOLE DAMA BIANCA

700 grams (1½ lbs) ripe, red strawberries
4 tablespoons orange liqueur
Caster sugar
2 egg whites
175 millilitres (6 fl. oz) double cream
½–1 teaspoon vanilla essence

Clean or wash strawberries. Drain off any excess moisture and hull them. In a serving bowl, mix strawberries lightly with liqueur and sweeten to taste with about 2 tablespoons sugar. Cover bowl and chill thoroughly by placing bowl in refrigerator for about 3 hours.

About 30 minutes before serving, beat egg whites until they stand in soft peaks. Beat in 75 grams (3 oz) caster sugar, a little at a time, and continue to beat to a stiff, glossy meringue. In another bowl, using the same beaters, beat cream with vanilla until it is very thick and beginning to stand in soft peaks. Fold meringue and cream together lightly until well blended.

Pile cream on strawberries and return bowl to refrigerator to chill lightly for 30 minutes.

Serves 6

COLONIAL SHORTCAKE

225 grams (8 oz) plain flour
3 teaspoons baking powder
Generous pinch of salt
2–3 tablespoons caster sugar
75 grams (3 oz) butter or white vegetable fat
Generous 150 millilitres (¼ pint) single cream or creamy milk

To finish
Softened butter
700–900 grams (1½–2 lbs) strawberries
Caster sugar
Lemon juice (optional)
Lightly whipped cream

To make shortcake, sift flour, baking powder, salt and
sugar into a bowl. Using your fingertips or 2 knives, work
in butter or vegetable fat until mixture resembles fine
breadcrumbs. Then, stirring with a knife blade, gradually
pour in enough cream or milk to make a very soft dough
that holds together. Turn it out on to a floured board and
knead very briefly (literally, a few times only). Pat dough

out into a 20 centimetre (8 in.) circle and place it on a buttered baking sheet, or fit it into a well-buttered layer cake tin that is 20 centimetres (8 in.) in diameter. Dot or spread surface with a tablespoon of softened butter.

Bake shortcake in a hot oven (230°C, 450°F, Mark 8) for about 15 minutes until well risen and nicely browned on top.

While shortcake is baking, clean and hull strawberries. Halve or slice half of them thickly, depending on size. Crush the remainder lightly with a fork. Sweeten the two portions of fruit with a little sugar and if liked add a few drops of lemon juice.

When shortcake is ready, turn it out on a cooling rack until it is just cool enough to handle. Then with a serrated knife, carefully split it in two horizontally. Spread cut surfaces generously with more softened butter.

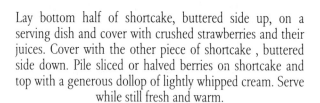

Lay bottom half of shortcake, buttered side up, on a serving dish and cover with crushed strawberries and their juices. Cover with the other piece of shortcake , buttered side down. Pile sliced or halved berries on shortcake and top with a generous dollop of lightly whipped cream. Serve while still fresh and warm.

Serves 4

STRAWBERRIES JUBILEE

900 grams (2 lbs) strawberries, fresh or frozen
75–125 grams (3–4 oz) caster sugar
150 millilitres (¼ pint) Kirsch or Maraschino liqueur
About 900 millilitres–1.1 litres (1½–2 pints) ice cream

If using fresh berries, clean and hull them, keeping them as dry as possible. Sweeten to taste with sugar and put aside for 30 minutes. Frozen berries should be sweetened according to whether they were packed with sugar or not, and allowed to defrost only to the stage where they are still very chilly and firm to the touch.

When the ice cream has been unmoulded, ready to serve, bring the liqueur to haze point in a wide, shallow pan. Have a long match ready. Keeping the heat under the pan high, tip in the strawberries and shake them around in the hot liqueur until the juices have evaporated sufficiently for the alcohol to ignite. Let the flames get a good hold.

Tip the flaming contents of the pan over the ice cream and serve the dessert at once.

Serves 6–8

CLASSIC STRAWBERRIES IN CREAM

450 grams (1 lb) ripe, even-sized strawberries, hulled
Finely grated rind and juice of 1 small sweet orange
4–6 tablespoons caster sugar
1 large carton 225 millilitres (about 8 fl. oz) whipping cream
1 small carton 150 millilitres (about 5 fl. oz) thick natural yoghourt

In a bowl, sprinkle strawberries with orange rind and juice, and a tablespoon of sugar, and mix lightly. Beat the cream until stiff but not buttery. In another bowl, beat yoghourt lightly until smooth. Fold whipped cream into yoghourt and sweeten with 3 tablespoons caster sugar. Fold strawberries and their juices into cream mixture, making sure they are individually coated, and sweeten with a little more sugar to taste if necessary. Spoon into a serving bowl and chill thoroughly.

Serves 4–6

FRESH STRAWBERRY FLAN

A flan made with fresh strawberries is quick and easy to
make and always delicious.

Make a tart shell with rich shortcrust pastry and when it is
cool fill it with strawberries. Pack them tightly together
with the pointed ends up. Make a glaze by melting 100–
125 grams (4 oz) smooth strawberry jam with a little water.
Strain the liquid, allow it to cool slightly, then spoon it
over the fruit.

FRENCH STRAWBERRY ICE CREAM

450 grams (1 lb) ripe red strawberries
Juice of 1 lemon
About 225 grams (8 oz) caster sugar
150 millilitres (¼ pint) double cream
Red food colouring (optional)
Whole strawberries or fresh puréed raspberry sauce, to serve

Clean and hull strawberries. In an electric blender or food processor, blend strawberries to a smooth purée. Blend in lemon juice, followed by enough sugar to give purée a strong, sweet flavour. (Remember that freezing will modify flavours, so use more lemon juice or sugar if necessary.)

In a bowl, beat cream until it thickens and begins to hold its shape softly. Gradually beat in strawberry purée. Add colouring if needed.

Pour into ice cube trays or a shallow plastic box. Cover with foil or a lid and freeze until ice cream has congealed around sides but is still soft and creamy in the middle.

Scrape mixture out into a bowl and beat vigorously until uniformly smooth and creamy once more (use an electric mixer for this if you have one).

Pour back into container(s). Cover and freeze until firm.

Transfer to main body of refrigerator for about 1 hour to soften slightly before serving.

Serve the ice cream with fresh whole strawberries, lightly sugared if necessary, or masked with a purée of fresh raspberries.

Serves 4–6

CHOCOLATE
STRAWBERRY JELLIES

900 grams (2 lbs) fresh, ripe strawberries
700 grams (1½ lbs) sugar
450 grams (1 lb) dark dipping (couverture) chocolate

Clean and hull the strawberries and wash in cold water, discarding any damaged berries. Purée by mashing or in an electric blender. Place the purée in a thick-bottomed saucepan. Stir in the sugar. Cook over a low heat, stirring constantly with a wooden spoon until the mixture is thick enough for a clean line to be left on the bottom of the pan when a spoon is drawn across it. Remove the pan from the heat.

Grease a large baking tray. Distribute the strawberry mixture in little mounds – about 1 heaped teaspoon of mixture in each – on the baking tray. Leave to set.

When each strawberry jelly is firm to touch, prepare the chocolate coating. Break the chocolate into small pieces and place in a bowl that will fit securely over a pan with hot water in it, without the water touching the bottom of the bowl.

Cover the bowl, and let the chocolate melt, stirring occasionally with a wooden spoon. When the chocolate has melted completely, beat until it is smooth and creamy. Place a sugar thermometer in the chocolate and leave it until the temperature has fallen to 43°C (110°F). At this temperature the chocolate should be of the right consistency for coating. A small amount picked up on a finger should set immediately.

Place the tray of strawberry jellies next to the bowl of chocolate. Line another, similar size, baking tray with waxed paper and place this on the other side of the bowl of chocolate. Drop the jellies, one at a time, into the chocolate. Use a fork to submerge and turn them. When well coated, lift out on the fork, tapping it on the side of the bowl to remove excess chocolate. Hold the fork over the tray lined with waxed paper and angle the fork so that the chocolate jelly rolls off. Make sure the jellies are well spaced. Leave for several hours until the chocolate is completely hard. Store between pieces of waxed paper in an air-tight container.

MERINGUE GATEAU

900 grams (2 lbs) strawberries
About 8 tablespoons icing sugar
6 tablespoons fruit liqueur
300 millilitres (½ pint) double cream, chilled
150 millilitres (¼ pint) single cream, chilled
6 meringues

Clean and hull strawberries. Pick out a dozen or so of the best specimens and put them aside for decoration. Chop remaining berries up roughly and put them in a bowl. Sift icing sugar, to taste, over the top. Sprinkle with liqueur or brandy if used. Mix lightly, cover and chill for 1 hour.

In another bowl, combine creams and beat until they hold their shape in soft peaks. Gently but thoroughly fold in chopped strawberries and all their juices. In the palm of your hand, crush each meringue into large pieces, dropping them on to strawberry cream. Fold into cream.

Taste and add more sugar if necessary.
Pile cream into a glass serving bowl, dot with reserved whole strawberries and serve.

Serves 6–8

STRAWBERRY PRESERVE

1.4 kilograms (3 lbs) strawberries
1.4 kilograms (3 lbs) sugar
Juice of 1 large or 2 small lemons, strained

Clean the strawberries if necessary and hull them. Lay them in a large, shallow dish and cover them evenly with 900 grams (2 lbs) sugar. Leave until the next day to allow sugar to draw out as much juice as possible.

Next day, pour off strawberry juices into a preserving pan, together with as much of the sugar as possible. Add the remaining 450 grams (1 lb) of sugar. Place pan over low heat until all the sugar has completely dissolved, stirring frequently.

Bring the syrup to the boil and slide in the strawberries all at once. Bring to boiling point again and boil until strawberries are nearly ready and turning translucent, swirling pan round frequently and skimming off the scum with a large spoon as necessary.

Then add the lemon juice and boil the jam until setting point is reached, shaking the pan frequently. Allow the jam to cool undisturbed in the preserving pan before potting and covering as usual.

Fills about 5 jars

Note: For a special luxury strawberry preserve, dip the hulled end of each strawberry into a saucerful of brandy as you prepare them. This is a favourite Middle Eastern trick.

STRAWBERRY FIELDS WINE

1.4 kilograms (3 lbs) ripe strawberries
450 grams (1 lb) ripe bananas
450 grams (1 lb) raisins, chopped
15 grams (½ oz) citric acid
1 teaspoon Pectozyme
1 Campden tablet
Madeira yeast
1.4 kilograms (3 lbs) demerara sugar

Clean and hull the strawberries and wash thoroughly under cold running water. Peel the bananas and chop coarsely. Heat 4 litres (7 pints) water to boiling point in a preserving pan. Put all the fruit including the raisins in the prepared mashing vessel and mash well together. Pour the hot water over the fruit, cover and allow to cool to 18°C (65°F). Then quickly stir in the citric acid, Pectozyme and Campden tablet. Cover the vessel. Leave for 24 hours.

Quickly, stir in the activated yeast (see manufacturer's instructions for quantity and method of use). No nutrient tablet is necessary in this recipe. Re-cover the vessel and leave in a warm place (18–24°C or 65–75°F) for 6 days. During this time, stir once a day to make sure the fruit is kept moist.

Using a fine sieve, strain off the liquid into a clean, sterile container. Put the fruit pulp into a linen bag. Seal the bag and squeeze out as much juice as possible into the strained liquid. Stir in the sugar. Quickly siphon into a fermenta-

tion vessel, filling to within 2.5 centimetres (1 in.) of the cork. Ferment in a warm, dark place (18–24°C or 65–75°F) under an airlock. This will take about 4 weeks. When a deep layer of sediment has formed on the bottom of the vessel, rack until clear.

Store the wine in a dark place for 6 months, then bottle. Leave for 2 years before drinking.

Makes 4.5 litres
(1 gal)

CHAMPAGNE COCKTAIL

6 strawberries
1 orange, peeled and sliced
3 tablespoons caster sugar
2 tablespoons lemon juice
100–125 millilitres (¼ pint) cognac
1 bottle champagne, well chilled

Chop the strawberries and orange very finely.
Sprinkle with the caster sugar and pour the lemon juice
and cognac over the fruit.
Chill the mixture for a minimum of an hour.
Immediately before serving, divide the mixture between 6
chilled champagne glasses. Fill the glasses with champagne
and serve.

Serves 6

STRAWBERRY VINEGAR

450 grams (1 lb) strawberries
550 millilitres (1 pint) white wine vinegar

Put the strawberries and vinegar in a glass or china bowl.
Cover with a clean cloth and leave for about 4 days. Stir
the mixture occasionally.
Strain through a sieve and measure the liquid. For each
550 millilitres (pint) allow 350 grams (12 oz) sugar.
Combine the two in an enamel or stainless steel pan. Bring
to the boil, stirring until the sugar has dissolved, and
continue boiling for 10 minutes longer.
Pour into hot bottles and seal.

HOT STRAWBERRY SAUCE

450 grams (1 lb) very ripe strawberries
350 grams (12 oz) sugar
3 tablespoons Kirsch

Clean and hull strawberries, and wash thoroughly in a colander under cold, running water. Make a purée by mashing the fruit with a fork or potato masher (or, ideally, use an electric blender). Leave the purée on one side.

In a thick-bottomed saucepan, heat the sugar and 300 millilitres (½ pint) water, stirring frequently, until boiling. Lower the heat and simmer, stirring occasionally, for about 20 minutes until the syrup thickens slightly. Leave to cool for a few moments before stirring in the strawberry purée and mixing thoroughly.

Just before serving, heat the mixture to desired temperature (do not boil). Remove from the heat, and stir in the Kirsch.

COSMETICS

Strawberries are universally recommended for the skin, especially the face. They have a mild astringent and bleaching effect, and are used in many masks and creams. Masks made from strawberries cleanse and refresh the skin, reduce oiliness, and lighten freckles. Mash berries that are too over-ripe to serve, pat or smear them on your face, and leave on as long as possible.

Strawberry juice can also be used on its own or with milk. Take a piece of linen or cotton roughly the size of your face, cut holes for eyes and mouth, soak it in the juice, wring out lightly and apply. As it dries, re-soak and re-apply.

PEARL AND PINK FACE CREAM

This light, creamy but not greasy, cream softens and tones the skin.

Take 1 part lanolin, 3 parts oil (almond, avocado, peach or olive), and 2 parts strawberry juice. Melt the lanolin in the oil in the top half of a double boiler. Remove from the heat and add the strawberry juice gradually, beating all the time until cool.

To make a large quantity, substitute up to 10 per cent of the oil with wheatgerm oil, to preserve it. Add the contents of a Vitamin E capsule (200 I.U.) for extra nourishment.

REMEDIES

Fresh strawberries are excellent for invalids and have been recommended for sufferers from liver complaints, gout and rheumatism.

Strawberry leaves and roots are often used to make a tea: use 2 tablespoons to 550 millilitres (1 pint) water. They can also be boiled in wine. This relieves diarrhoea and dysentery, problems of the liver and urinary tract, and is recommended for heavy periods.

An infusion of strawberry leaves can be used as a mouthwash to strengthen gums and freshen the breath. It makes a good gargle for sore throats and mouth ulcers (and can be used as a compress for ulcers and sores anywhere).

The juice removes tartar from the teeth, and the leaves can be dried, powdered finely, sprinkled on a dry toothbrush and used, very effectively, as a toothpowder. The root may also be used; equal quantities of dried, powdered sage are a good addition. Brushing with this mixture stimulates and strengthens the gums

MEASUREMENTS

Quantities have been given in both metric and imperial measures in this book. However, many foodstuffs are now available only in metric quantities; the list below gives metric measures for weight and liquid capacity, and their imperial equivalents used in this book.

WEIGHT

25 grams	1 oz
50 grams	2 oz
75 grams	3 oz
100–125 grams	4 oz
150 grams	5 oz
175 grams	6 oz
200 grams	7 oz
225 grams	8 oz
250 grams	9 oz
275 grams	10 oz
300 grams	11 oz
350 grams	12 oz
375 grams	13 oz

400 grams	14 oz
425 grams	15 oz
450 grams	1 lb
500 grams (½ kilogram)	1 lb 1½ oz
1 kilogram	2 lb 3 oz
1.5 kilograms	3 lb 5 oz
2 kilograms	4 lb 6 oz
2.5 kilograms	5 lb 8 oz
3 kilograms	6 lb 10 oz
3.5 kilograms	7 lb 11 oz
4 kilograms	8 lb 13 oz
4.5 kilograms	9 lb 14 oz
5 kilograms	11 lb

LIQUID CAPACITY

150 millilitres	¼ pint
300 millilitres	½ pint
425 millilitres	¾ pint
550–600 millilitres	1 pint
900 millilitres	1½ pints
1000 millilitres (1 litre)	1¾ pints
1.2 litres	2 pints
1.3 litres	2¼ pints
1.4 litres	2½ pints
1.5 litres	2¾ pints
1.9 litres	3¼ pints
2 litres	3½ pints
2.5 litres	4½ pints

OVEN TEMPERATURES

Very low	130°C, 250°F, Mark ½
Low	140°C, 275°F, Mark 1
Very slow	150°C, 300°F, Mark 2
Slow	170°C, 325°F, Mark 3
Moderate	180°C, 350°F, Mark 4
	190°C, 375°F, Mark 5
Moderately hot	200°C, 400°F, Mark 6
Fairly hot	220°C, 425°F, Mark 7
Hot	230°C, 450°F, Mark 8